Idiom Tales

Teaching Guide

SCHOLASTIC

New York ○ Toronto ○ London ○ Auckland ○ Sydney
New Delhi ○ Mexico City ○ Hong Kong ○ Buenos Aires

Teaching *Resources*

Guide written by Pamela Chanko
Cover design by Maria Lilja
Interior design by Grafica, Inc.

ISBN-13: 978-0-545-21206-9 / ISBN-10: 0-545-21206-5

Table of Contents

Mini-Books and Activity Sheets

Introduction

Welcome to Idiom Tales, the program that helps you teach essential figures of speech in a snap—and have tons of fun doing it! Idioms can liven up students' writing, fine-tune verbal communication skills, and inspire creative thinking, not to mention the boost they give to reading comprehension. In many literacy programs, however, idioms can be given short shrift. With teachers under pressure to cover so many skills in so little time, every moment of the day counts. So it's understandable to ask, "Is teaching idioms really a must?" But if you want an answer to that question, start by answering this one: How many idioms have you counted in this paragraph?

If you counted more than five, you probably already know what a crucial role idioms play in our language. Many people think of idioms as mere slang, but this is not the case. An idiom is any group of words whose meaning is different from the definitions of the individual words. That is, the phrase as a whole has a figurative interpretation that differs from the literal definition. Some idioms are so common that we barely notice them. For example, when you read the first sentence on this page, did you wonder what kind of scale you'd have to use to weigh "fun," particularly "tons" of it? Did you get out your stopwatch to see just how much time went by "in a snap" of your fingers? Of course not! Your brain automatically translated these phrases into the ideas they have come to represent. But you weren't born with this ability; you had to learn it. That's why studying idioms is an essential component of any balanced literacy curriculum. First, students learned how letters—which represent sounds—could be put together in special ways to form words—which represent concepts. Now they are ready to learn that words can be put together in special ways to represent meanings—and that those meanings aren't always what they seem!

The Idiom Tales program introduces students to groups of related idioms by putting them in the context of engaging stories. Each story in the collection focuses on a particular type of idiom, for instance: *True Colors* features idioms related to color; *Peas in a Pod* introduces idioms that reference food; *The Wild-Goose Chase* teaches idioms about animals. Through lovable characters and high-interest plots, students not only learn specific idioms, but they also learn to see language itself in a whole new way. The program shows students that English is not just a static, "boring" set of rules that must be learned; instead, it is a living, ever-changing entity with its own amazing history, culture, and secrets. In fact, Idiom Tales gives even the most reluctant students something to love about language: the fact that its rules can sometimes be broken! With a solid vocabulary and a little creativity, students might even make up some idioms of their own. So what are you waiting for? It's time you taught students how to read between the lines. Now get with the program and hit the books! With Idiom Tales, it'll be a piece of cake.

How to Use the Program

The Idiom Tales program is designed to fit easily into any teacher's classroom. With super-flexible components, you can add just a sprinkling of idioms to your curriculum, or go the whole nine yards with a comprehensive study. It's all up to you!

Choosing an Instructional Sequence

Idioms can be classified into two basic categories: "transparent" and "opaque." Transparent idioms are easier to understand because the figurative meaning is closely connected to the literal words. Opaque idioms are more difficult because the words don't give much of a clue to the figurative meaning. For example, if you describe two people as *fighting like cats and dogs*, anyone with prior knowledge of these animals' typical behavior will probably get the meaning; this idiom is fairly transparent. If you say that the two later *buried the hatchet*, however, only someone who knows the idiom will be likely to understand; this idiom is more opaque.

There's no "wrong" order for teaching the idioms presented in the program, but this guide is loosely structured along a continuum from transparent to opaque idioms. For instance, idioms about animals come first because animal traits tend to be universally recognized: it's fairly easy to form a mental image of what a *wild-goose chase* or a *sly fox* might look like and, therefore, to understand these idioms. The same is true for expressions about the human body—everybody has one, so idiomatic metaphors like *long face* and *heart of gold* are fairly clear. Food idioms (such as *in a pickle* or *smart cookie*) tend to be less transparent, so this category is placed toward the end of the guide. Sports idioms are presented last because they require knowledge of particular sports; so while these idioms may seem transparent to some, they may be opaque to others.

Of course, it's important to keep in mind that you're the best judge of what your students will relate to best. If you've got a class full of athletes, you might want to read *Slam Dunk!* first rather than last. Students with an artistic bent might connect most to the idioms in *True Colors*. Every storybook in the program spotlights a unique way of expressing ideas, and each group of idioms has an important place in our language. So whatever sequence you choose, Idiom Tales will add loads of value—as well as loads of fun—to your curriculum!

Program Components

Everything you need to implement the Idiom Tales program in your classroom is right inside the handy storage box. Here's a quick guide to each teaching tool.

Storybooks Each of the eight full-color storybooks focuses on a different idiom category, including animals, weather, clothing, food, and more. This is a great way to teach idiomatic expressions because it builds content vocabulary at the same time. For example, as students learn sports idioms, they're practicing action words such as *swing*, *skate*, and *kick*. They're also learning how the literal meanings of these words contribute to figurative expressions, adding a new dimension to their vocabulary. The idioms play a natural part in each story, providing ample context for their meanings. Some stories also include rhyme, highlighting the lively qualities of language even more. The playful illustrations also contribute to the fun—they depict both the literal and figurative meanings of each idiom simultaneously! Additional educational elements of each book include boldface print to call out each idiom, a Learning Box explaining the idiom's meaning and origin, and a matching activity and extension idea on the last page. For specific tips on making the most of the storybooks, turn to page 8 of this guide.

Mini-Books Included in this guide is a reproducible mini-book version of each Idiom Tale in the program. The mini-books are unabridged replicas of the full-size books, so each student can build a personal library! They're terrific for independent, small-group, and take-home activities. See page 11 for mini-book ideas.

Activity Sheets Following each mini-book, you'll find two reproducible activity sheets to reinforce and expand on the idioms students have just learned. The activity sheets are designed to keep interest high by including fun puzzles, "secret" codes to crack, and characters from the stories. Many of the activity sheets are self-checking, but you'll also find a convenient answer key at the back of this guide. Each Idiom Tale is accompanied by two types of activity sheets:

- **Reinforcement Activity Sheets** The first sheet following each mini-book reinforces students' grasp of the idioms presented in the storybook. Activities include using the idioms to complete crossword clues, unscrambling words in the idioms to read a secret message, and using the idioms to complete new stories about the characters.

- **Supplementary Activity Sheets** The second sheet following each mini-book expands students' knowledge by teaching additional idioms from the same category. The sheets provide plenty of clues for students to figure out the meanings of these new expressions—plus, each puzzle has a built-in reward for finding the correct solution! Activities include choosing correct definitions for the idioms in a story to crack a code, matching idioms to their explanations to see a secret password, and searching for the words that make up an idiom to reveal that idiom's definition.

Activities to Extend Learning In addition to the pencil-and-paper activities, you'll find ideas for hands-on learning beginning on page 12 of this guide. By incorporating art, movement, and creative thinking, these activities will help you make idioms jump off the page and spring to life!

Using the Program With English Language Learners

Teaching idioms takes on special importance with ELL students. Many idioms are challenging even for native English speakers, so they can be particularly confusing to those just learning the language. Use these tips to scaffold students' learning.

Pre-Teach Many ELL's benefit from small-group mini-lessons prior to whole-class instruction. Review each idiom in the story, providing students with the definition and discussing examples. For students who need additional help, you might read the whole book, substituting each idiom's definition in the idiom's place. This way, students will have a firm grasp of the story before exploring the abstract expressions.

Compare/Contrast Most idioms are culturally unique; that is, the idioms used in one country do not usually translate word-for-word to another. However, there are quite a few idioms that have basic equivalents across many languages. For instance, the Spanish version of the English idiom *between a rock and a hard place* translates literally as "between the wall and the sword." Italians multi-task by *trapping two pigeons with one bean*, while Americans save time by *killing two birds with one stone*. Invite ELL students to share idioms from their native language, and challenge the class to find similar expressions in English.

Either/Or The best way for ELL students to begin understanding idioms is to start using them—but their level of language production can be an impediment. One way to get around this problem is by giving students a choice of idioms and having them echo the one they think makes sense. Set up a context and then ask students a question with an embedded answer, for example: "If you're spending the day listening to music and talking with friends, are you *chilling out* or *chasing rainbows*?" When students tell you they're *chilling out*, they're also using idioms!

Teachable Moments Helping students connect idioms to everyday experiences can make idioms seem less abstract. For instance, if you see an ELL student spending a lot of time with one classmate, you can say: *You two are such close friends, it's as if you were joined at the hip!* When a student produces good work, you can observe: *This is terrific. You should be proud as a peacock!* In fact, teachable moments might just be the most convenient teaching tools around—they can occur in any learning environment and under virtually any circumstances, and still make an impact. So the next time students' fidgeting is *driving you up the wall*, take advantage and comment on the *ants in their pants* before telling them to *buckle down!*

Connections to the Language Arts Standards

The books and activities in this program are designed to support you in meeting the following standards for students in grades 3–5, outlined by Mid-continent Research for Education and Learning (McREL), an organization that collects and synthesizes national and state K–12 curriculum standards.

Uses the general skills and strategies of the writing process:
- Writes in response to literature

Uses the stylistic and rhetorical aspects of writing:
- Uses descriptive language that clarifies and enhances ideas, such as common figures of speech

Uses the general skills and strategies of the reading process:
- Uses a variety of context clues to decode unknown words
- Uses reference materials to determine the meanings and derivations of unknown words
- Understands level-appropriate reading vocabulary such as multi-meaning words

Uses reading skills and strategies to understand a variety of literary texts:
- Understands the ways in which language is used in literary texts, such as personification, simile, metaphor, imagery, and hyperbole

Uses reading skills and strategies to understand a variety of informational texts:
- Uses text organizers such as graphic features and typeface to locate information in a text
- Uses the various parts of a book to locate information
- Uses prior knowledge and experience to understand and respond to new information

Uses listening and speaking strategies for different purposes:
- Uses level-appropriate vocabulary in speech, such as familiar idioms, similes, and word play
- Understands that language reflects different regions and cultures, such as sayings, expressions, and usage; understands historical and societal influences on language

Source: *Content Knowledge: A Compendium of Standards and Benchmarks for K–12 Education. 4th edition* (Mid-continent Research for Education and Learning, 2004)

Making the Most of the Storybooks

The playful stories in the Idiom Tales program are bound to be a hit for any read-aloud, at any time—but that's just the tip of the iceberg. There's also a virtual storehouse of learning opportunities embedded within each tale! The following tips can maximize students' experiences before, during, and after reading. Choose a few or use them all to create customized literacy lessons that fit your classroom to a tee!

Before Reading

◎ Before you read your first Idiom Tale, find out how much students know about figures of speech. Choose an idiom that has both a literal and figurative meaning and write two example sentences on the board, for instance:

> *My brother was making too much noise, so I told him to cut it out.*

> *My brother saw a coupon in a magazine for a free video game, so he cut it out.*

◎ Ask students what the underlined words mean in each sentence (*to stop doing something; to remove something with scissors*). Explain that in the first sentence, the phrase *cut it out* is an idiom. An idiom—also called a saying or an expression—is a combination of words that has a different meaning from the meanings of the individual words. Discuss a few more everyday idioms (such as *lend a hand* or *catch cold*) and invite students to share any others they know.

◎ Display the cover of the book and read the title. Then point out the label in the upper right corner and read the text aloud. Ask students if they know any expressions that would fit in the category (such as *chicken out* or *quiet as a mouse* for Sayings About Animals). Then explain that in the story, students will see lots of idioms related to the same topic—in fact, even the title is an idiom! Can students guess what it means? Encourage them to look at the cover illustration for clues.

◎ Next, use the cover as a springboard for story-related discussion. Encourage students to make predictions about the plot and characters based on the illustration. For instance, when previewing *The Wild-Goose Chase*, you might ask: *What is the girl holding? Do her clothes give you an idea of who she is and what she does? Why do you think she is running?* If you like, you can write students' predictions on the board and revisit them after reading.

During Reading

◎ The first time you share each book with students, read only the main text, the story itself. Explain that students may hear some unfamiliar expressions (and see some wacky pictures), but there will be plenty of time to talk about them afterward. Read the book straight through, as you would any other story. This way, students can experience the flow of the language and the imagery it helps create. It will also help students to enjoy the story for the plot, the characters, and the illustrations.

◉ Once students have heard the story and "met" the characters, you can go back and explore the idioms. Focusing on one boldface phrase at a time, ask: *What do you think this idiom means? Why do you think so?* Encourage students to use context clues and story knowledge to draw their conclusions. For instance, while reading *Every Cloud Has a Silver Lining*, you might help students analyze the idiom on page 6 of the story by asking: *Do you think the Thompson triplets want to win the talent show? Will they be disappointed if Darla gets the prize? How is their situation similar to having rainy weather on the day of a parade? Would that be disappointing, too?*

◉ After giving students a chance to make inferences about each idiom, read the text in the Learning Box. Take time to discuss the etymological information—the definition of an idiom is sometimes much clearer once you understand how the expression came to be. For instance, the expression *behind the eight ball* (used in *Slam Dunk!*) makes very little sense until you learn the rules of the billiards game on which the saying is based. Besides, the origins of some idioms are so interesting that they're just plain fun to read about. For example, sharing the background behind the expression *dog-tired* (on page 14 of *Over the Moon*) is like reading students a whole new story—a bite-sized one that fits right in the Learning Box!

◉ After discussing the text with students, take some time to appreciate the illustrations. Ask: *What do you notice about these pictures? How are they different from pictures in other stories?* Lead students to see that each picture not only helps illustrate what's happening in the story, but also shows a literal depiction of the idiom on that page. For example, in *Over the Moon*, Matt McKay is shown literally lying beneath a storm cloud when he is *under the weather*. In *The Long Arm of the Law*, the card player's hair has caught fire because he's such a *hothead*. These exaggerated details don't represent actual events in the story, but they sure are fun to look at! Use the literal aspects of the illustrations to bring home the vivid imagery that idioms can create.

◉ Next, discuss how the illustrations also show the figurative meaning of each idiom: that is, what the phrase means when taken as a whole. For instance, when looking at the illustrations mentioned above, students can see that Matt is under the weather from his unhappy face and from the fact that he's in bed. And as for the card player, they can tell he's a hothead because his face is incredibly angry—in fact, he's such a sore loser that he's throwing his cards up in the air!

After Reading

◉ After reading each book, encourage students to play the Idiom Match game on page 16. You can have each student use a separate sheet of paper to complete the activity, or work on it all together. You'll find the correct answers in upside-down print beneath the activity.

◉ Of course, there's more to knowing an idiom than just being able to define it—when it comes to idioms, you can't walk the walk without talking the talk! After students match the idioms with their correct definitions, you might want to check their understanding by having them use each one in a new context. Students can use the idioms in made-up sentences, share experiences they've had to which the idioms apply, or tell about a time when knowing a particular expression might have come in handy! For example, when discussing the idioms in *True Colors*, a student might say: *I was purple with rage when my brother made a mess and blamed it on me. He was yellow-bellied for not admitting the truth!*

◉ In each book, you'll find an extra mini-activity beneath the Idiom Match game on page 16. Each one encourages students to "go the extra mile" and explore the idiom category even further. For instance, students are asked to describe fictional characters using food idioms after reading *Peas in a Pod*. At the end of *The Wild-Goose Chase*, students are challenged to make up five new idioms about animals. You can have students complete these activities independently during school time, or you can assign them as homework. Of course, you can also do the activities with small groups or the whole class.

◉ For a fun wrap-up, invite students to write a literature response in the form of a book review. They can express both positive and negative reactions they had to the story, with just one catch: they must use at least three idioms in their review! Tell students their idioms don't have to come from the book, but they do need to belong to the same category. For instance, a review of *Slam Dunk!* might be: *I had to read this story a few times to get the hang of all the idioms, but then I sailed through it. I thought Timmy's parents were kind of impatient for making him race against the clock, but it was fun to see how he did it! I thought the story was a slam-dunk.*

◉ For more practice with the idioms from the story, use the activity sheet directly following the mini-book in this guide. And remember, there's an extra sheet for each title, which will help students learn even more idioms. You can also follow up your storybook reading with any of the activities on pages 12–14 of this guide. These fun, easy ideas will reinforce students' new knowledge by providing hands-on experiences.

◉ After giving students multiple experiences with the story, there's also a follow-up activity for you to do: stand back and listen up! You might just start hearing some lively, colorful new language in your classroom each day. After all, that's one of the best parts of teaching a good lesson on idioms—the results really do speak for themselves!

Making and Using the Mini-Books

Follow these tips to create the mini-books and use them both in and out of the classroom.

How to Assemble the Mini-Books

1. Make double-sided copies of the mini-book pages. (You should have two double-sided copies for each one.)

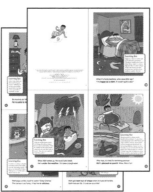

2. Stack the pages and cut them across the horizontal dotted line. Do not cut along the solid line.

3. Position the pages with lettered spreads (A, B, C, D) faceup. Place the B spread on top of the A spread. Then, place the C and D spreads on top of those in sequence.

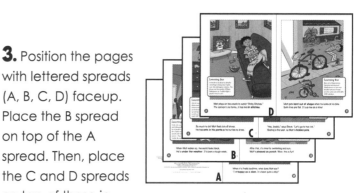

4. Fold the pages in half along the solid line. Make sure all the pages are in the correct order. Then staple them together along the book's spine.

How to Use the Mini-Books

Learning Centers Creating learning centers with the mini-books is a cinch! As you focus on each idiom category, build a center around it by adding copies of the mini-book and the associated worksheets. You can also place themed stationery in the center and ask students to write their own paragraph or story using the idioms. In addition, you might provide books, magazines, and newspapers, and challenge students to find examples of idioms that belong to the category in real-world text.

Group Reading Students can use their mini-books to follow along silently as you read the storybook aloud, or to participate in shared-reading activities, such as echo reading and choral reading. The mini-books can also be used for small-group lessons, such as guided reading, and for fluency practice activities, such as reader's theater.

Idiom Reference Libraries Students can collect all eight mini-books and place them in a pocket portfolio or file box to create a mini-library! The books are fun to read for pure enjoyment, but they will also come in handy when students need a colorful phrase to liven up one of their own stories, poems, or reports.

Idiom Tales Teaching Guide • 11

Family Involvement Send copies of the mini-books home with students and invite parents to join in the fun. After family members read the book with their child, you can have them do a quick activity together, such as listening for idioms in song lyrics or on TV.

Activities to Extend Learning

These fun ideas can be used with the sayings children learn through the Idiom Tales program as well as with any other idiomatic expressions you'd like to introduce.

Drawing Things Out
Combine art with idioms for some interesting results!

◉ The illustrations in Idiom Tales show a literal interpretation of each idiom—now it's students' turn! Provide paper and markers or crayons and have each student select an idiom to draw. Students might choose an idiom from the story (to be illustrated in a new way), an idiom they learned from the activity sheets, or any other idiom they know.

◉ If you like, create a sample illustration for students. For instance, you might draw someone hanging from a tree branch for *out on a limb*, or draw a person with an armful of musical notes for *carry a tune*. Then have students create their own drawings. Tell them they can use speech bubbles and words in their illustrations (for example, *drop a hint* might be depicted by someone dropping the word *hint*), but they should not write out the whole expression.

◉ When students are finished, use the illustrations to create an interactive display. For an easier activity, have students write their idioms on a separate sentence strip, then post the pictures and strips in mixed-up order, and invite students to match each illustration with the correct idiom. For a greater challenge, have students write their idioms on the back of their drawings and try to name one another's idioms from the illustrations alone. They can then turn over the picture to check their guess!

You're Pulling My Leg!
Invite students to learn—and invent—origins of popular idioms.

◉ Because idiomatic expressions are so colorful, they often have colorful—but untrue—stories attached to them. These rumored origins are called false etymologies. For example, some people say the idiom *give the cold shoulder* (meaning "treat with disdain") originally referred to a cut of meat! According to the story, visitors who were welcome in a home got a hot meal, while unwanted guests were given "the cold shoulder of mutton." This story *sounds* true, but research proves otherwise. The phrase actually first appeared in a novel, and was used to describe a character who coldly turned her back to someone. The shoulder she "gave" was most certainly a human one!

◉ Share the above false etymology with students, and look up more examples if you like. Then have students pair up to create their own false etymologies. Give each pair an idiom with a known origin, or have students choose one from an idiom dictionary. Encourage pairs to make up a story that explains the idiom: the more realistic, the better. For instance, students might say the expression *turn over a new leaf* (meaning "make a fresh start") comes from the days before calendars. The only way to tell the season had changed was to look at both sides of the new leaves on the trees! (In actuality, the "leaf" in this saying refers to a page in a book; in the original expression, it was most likely a book of lessons.)

◉ Let each pair present both the true and untrue origins of their idiom to the class, either orally or in written form. Then have the group vote on which story they think is true and which is false. To add a competitive edge, you might give a point to pairs who manage to "pull their classmates' legs" successfully!

The Writing on the Wall

Invite students to collect idioms from everyday contexts.

◉ Idioms are all around us—so much so that we often don't even notice them! In just one day, a sportscaster may tell us that our favorite team is *taking the lead*; the local paper may report that plans for a new shopping mall are *in the works*; and a parent may warn that homework shouldn't be *left to the last minute*. Set aside a special bulletin board for collecting common idioms like these, as well as less familiar expressions students may encounter. Together, brainstorm an idiomatic title for your board, such as "Idioms We *Caught Red-Handed!*

◉ Then encourage students to stay on the lookout for idioms, both in and out of school. For instance, students might bring in a newspaper or magazine clipping, copy an excerpt from a book, or write down idioms heard on TV or in conversations. When students bring in an idiom for the board, they should be prepared to explain the context in which it was used, and write a simple definition on an index card to be posted beneath.

◉ If you like, you can set a target number of idioms for the class to collect over a certain period of time. If students reach the goal, give them a special treat to reward their efforts!

Mind Your Business

Invite students to advertise a product with idioms!

◉ Advertising relies a lot on idioms and word play to sell products. For example, a certain brand of sugar might make baking *as easy as pie*, or a particular MP3 player might be *music to your ears*. Gather some magazines and newspapers and work with students to find examples of ads that use idioms.

◉ Next, divide the class into small groups and have each group come up with a product. It can be something they invent, such as a new brand of cereal, or an existing product they enjoy using. Encourage each group to brainstorm several idioms that relate to the product, using the storybooks for reference if they like. For instance, if students are advertising a food, they can look at *Peas in a Pod*; if their product is a piece of sports equipment, *Slam Dunk!* can provide a good starting point.

◉ Once students choose the idiom or idioms that will sell their product best, they can create an illustrated poster. Puns can make very catchy slogans, so encourage students to use word play if possible. For example, one ad might read: *With a PortaBuzz cell phone, there's no such thing as small talk!* Another might say: *Chip away at your hunger with Cheesy Crisps!* When groups are finished, invite them to share their posters with the class.

By the Same Token

Students can keep a log of idiomatic synonyms to spice up their writing.

◉ In the storybooks, students learned idioms according to category—animal idioms, color idioms, and so on. Another helpful way to group idioms is by what they mean. Introduce the concept of "idiom synonyms" by writing a word on the board, such as *walk*. Then brainstorm related idioms, for instance: *walk on eggshells*, *walk the plank*, *walk a fine line*, *walk in the park*, *walk on air*, and so on. Discuss how these expressions have different connotations, but share the same essential concept: walking.

◉ Now encourage students to begin their own idiom thesaurus in a journal or notebook. You can start them off with a few simple words or concepts, such as speed (*fast, slow*), looks (*pretty, cute, ugly*), and character traits (*smart, sweet, shy, loud*). Students can create a page for each concept and its associated idioms. They might start out with idioms from the storybooks and move on to adding idioms from an idiom dictionary.

◉ Encourage students to keep adding to their thesaurus as they hear new expressions, and to use it as a reference to make their own stories and poems more colorful.

Idiom Match

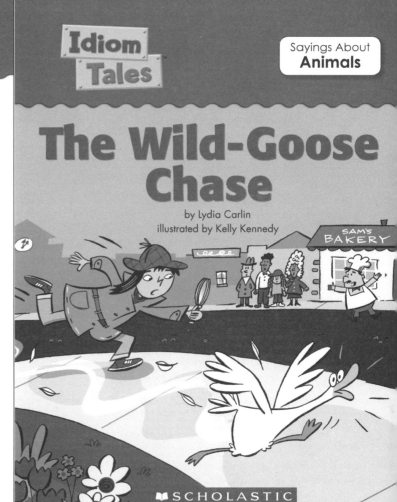

On a separate sheet of paper, match each idiom with its meaning.

1. horse around
2. eagle eyes
3. busy beaver
4. monkey business
5. sly fox
6. high-tail
7. proud as a peacock

8. pig out
9. hopping mad
10. wild-goose chase
11. cool cat
12. have a whale of a time

A. clever and sneaky
B. brimming with self-confidence
C. have a large amount of fun
D. move in a great hurry
E. someone who works very hard
F. eat a lot
G. a situation that's hopeless and confused
H. someone who is stylish and relaxed
I. goofy or naughty behavior
J. act silly in a playful way
K. eyes that see everything
L. very angry

Answer: 1-J, 2-K, 3-E, 4-I, 5-A, 6-D, 7-B, 8-F, 9-L, 10-G, 11-H, 12-C

Go the Extra Mile!

Here are five animals: chameleon, chimpanzee, mosquito, parrot, and sloth. For each animal, fill in the blank: "_____ *as a chameleon,*" for example. When you're done, pat yourself on the back. You made up five awesome idioms!

The Wild-Goose Chase

by Lydia Carlin
illustrated by Kelly Kennedy

SCHOLASTIC

Learning Box

Monkey business is a term used to describe goofy or naughty behavior. Other monkey-related idioms include *more fun than a barrel of monkeys* and *I'll be a monkey's uncle.*

I raced right over to the bakery and told Sam my theory. "I knew somebody was up to some **monkey business**. I just didn't know it was me," he said. Then he added, "I guess that explains why I woke up this morning with purple lips and a terrible tummy ache."

Learning Box

Idioms are well-known phrases that mean something different from what the words actually say. Idioms use lively and colorful language to conjure up images in the reader's mind. For that reason, they are remembered and often passed down from generation to generation. *Hungry as a bear* and *quiet as a mouse* are two popular animal idioms. Read on to learn 12 more!

Hi there! I'm Shirley Holmes and I'm a kid detective. Let me tell you about my latest case.

Designed by Grafica, Inc.
ISBN-13: 978-0-545-13482-8 • ISBN-10: 0-545-13482-X
Copyright © 2009 by Lefty's Editorial Services.
All rights reserved. Printed in China
SCHOLASTIC and associated logos are trademarks and/or registered trademarks of Scholastic Inc.

First printing, September 2009

12 11 10 9 8 7 6 5 4 3 2 1   9 10 11 12 13 14/0

A

Learning Box

Proud as a peacock is used to describe someone who is brimming with self-confidence. With feathers fanned out, peacocks sure look proud. This vivid idiom is one of the oldest in the English language and was used in the 1300s by the famous writer Geoffrey Chaucer.

Case closed. Sam was happy to learn there wasn't a pie thief on the loose after all. And I was happy, too. I had just solved another mystery. I guess you could say I was **proud as a peacock**!

Learning Box

Hopping mad is an idiom that's used when a person is angry enough to jump into the air. What kind of animal is famous for hopping? A frog, of course!

It all started with a frantic call from Sam Crumpet, who told me to come right over. When I arrived at his bakery, he gave me the facts. Last night, as he snoozed on a cot in the kitchen, someone snuck in and ate his freshly baked blueberry pie. Now Sam was **hopping mad**.

B

Learning Box

Pig out means to eat a great deal of food. Why? Among animals, pigs have a bad reputation for overeating. *Pig out* is an example of a modern idiom. The phrase was invented in the 1970s.

That's it! Sam must have sleepwalked from the kitchen to the front of the bakery and **pigged out** on the blueberry pie himself.

Learning Box

Eagle eyes is an idiom used to describe a person who sees everything. What does that have to do with eagles? These remarkable birds can spot prey that's a half mile away!

Luckily, I ran into a woman named Wanda Winger. Wanda was famous for her **eagle eyes**. She lived right next door to Sam's Bakery and had some important information to share. "I saw Sam sleepwalking last night," she said.

Learning Box

Busy beaver is an idiom that describes someone who works extremely hard. Why? Beavers cut down trees, haul logs, build dams, and always appear to be very active.

I began working on the case right away. I interviewed Sam. I examined the crime scene. I made a list of top suspects. Yup, I was one **busy beaver**.

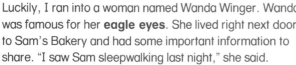

Learning Box

To have a *whale of a time* means to have a large amount of fun. The idiom makes a lot of sense because whales are playful creatures. They are also the largest animals on earth.

I arrived to find Barry in his backyard pool having a **whale of a time**. It was true he had a passion for pies. In fact, he loves every kind except one—blueberry. The reason? Apparently, that little blue fruit makes him break out in red spots. Clearly, Barry's not the pie thief.

Learning Box

Cool cat is an idiom that describes someone who is stylish and relaxed. Cats do seem like super-cool creatures, don't they?

My second suspect was a kid named Mack McClaw. Why? He was a **cool cat** with a weakness for delicious desserts. But Mack had an excuse, too. Last night, he was busy playing the sax. "You can even ask my band mates," he said.

Learning Box

Sly fox is an idiom used to describe someone who is clever and sneaky. Foxes, who are quick and quiet, have been perceived this way for hundreds of years. *The Gingerbread Boy*, *The Fox and the Grapes*—just think of all the folktales that include sly-fox characters!

My first suspect was a boy named Frankie Frisk. My reasoning? He was a **sly fox** and he loved sweet treats. But Frankie didn't do it. In fact, he was home all last night reading a cake cookbook. "You can even ask my mother," he said.

C

Learning Box

Wild-goose chase is an idiom that describes a situation that's hopeless and confused. Imagine how hard it would be to chase after a wild goose. Back in 1597, William Shakespeare used the phrase in his play *Romeo and Juliet*.

Hmmm. If it wasn't Frankie Frisk or Mack McClaw or Nellie Nay or Barry Beluga—then who ate Sam's freshly baked blueberry pie? This case was beginning to feel like a **wild-goose chase**!

Learning Box

Horse around means to act in a silly and playful way. Long ago, farmers noticed that their horses would sometimes get in giddy moods, in which they would whinny and prance about. The idiom *horseplay* is based on this same observation.

My third suspect was a girl named Nellie Nay. She was always **horsing around** and playing silly pranks. But she didn't eat the pie either. "Last night, I went to a movie with Helen Hoof," she said. Then she told me to check out a kid named Barry Beluga. It seemed that Barry was a fruit-pie fanatic.

D

Learning Box

High-tail is an idiom that means to move in a great hurry. This phrase is based on the behavior of deer. Why? When they run, they raise their tails as a sign of danger.

Hmmm. That sounded like a solid lead. So I **high-tailed** it over to Barry's house to hear what he had to say.

Shirley Holmes, Animal Detective

Help Shirley track down the animals that fit each clue.

**Choose a word from the box to complete each sentence correctly.
Then write your answers in the crossword puzzle.**

peacock	horse
monkey	beaver
eagle	whale
goose	cat
fox	pig

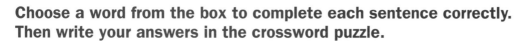

Across

2. Someone who's clever and sneaky
is a sly _____.

5. Someone who works extremely hard
is a busy _____.

7. A situation that's hopeless and
confused is a wild-_____ chase.

8. Someone who's brimming with self-
confidence is proud as a _____.

Down

1. To act silly in a playful way is to _____
around.

3. To have a large amount of fun is to
have a _____ of a time.

4. Someone who sees everything has
_____ eyes.

6. Goofy or naughty behavior is _____
business.

8. To eat a lot is to _____ out.

9. Someone who's stylish and relaxed is
a cool _____.

Animal Crackers!

Be a code cracker and help Shirley discover more animal idioms.

There are two definitions for the underlined idiom in each sentence below, but only one is correct! Read the sentence. Then circle the letter next to the correct answer.

1. Shirley Holmes paid close attention to everything her neighbors did. She <u>watched them like a hawk.</u>
   - **A.** watched them from a high branch on a tree
   - **B.** watched them very carefully

2. Shirley watched the bakery especially closely. She never knew when someone might <u>wolf down</u> another pie!
   - **E.** eat something very quickly and in large bites
   - **F.** follow something downhill

3. Shirley was guarding the bakery when a big thunderstorm started. "Come inside!" said Sam. "It's <u>raining cats and dogs</u>!"
   - **K.** raining extremely hard
   - **L.** scaring the animals

4. Shirley tried to answer, but a cough came out instead. "Excuse me," said Shirley. "I <u>had a frog in my throat</u>."
   - **M.** had a happy, jumpy feeling
   - **N.** had a hoarse voice or a need to clear the throat

5. "I hope you're not getting a cold," said Sam. He gave her a blanket and a slice of warm apple pie. Shirley was <u>snug as a bug in a rug</u>!
   - **R.** feeling cramped from being squeezed too tightly
   - **S.** feeling comfortable and warm

Now crack the code! Each number below stands for one of the questions. Write the letter of your answer above the number. Then read the message to see how Shirley feels about animals!

She thinks they're the

___ ___ ___ ___ ,   ___ ___ ___ ___ ___ ___ !
 1   2   2   5   3   4   2   2   5

Hint!

The answer is another animal idiom! Can you guess what it means?

Idiom Match

On a separate sheet of paper, match each idiom with its meaning.

1. butterfingers
2. stay on your toes
3. the long arm of the law
4. put your foot in your mouth
5. hothead
6. bury your head in the sand
7. long face
8. green thumb
9. chip on your shoulder
10. heart of gold
11. wet behind the ears
12. joined at the hip

A. say the wrong thing
B. stay alert
C. young and inexperienced
D. extremely kind
E. good at growing plants
F. sheriffs and police officers
G. clumsy with your hands
H. hide from danger
I. super-close
J. ready for a fight
K. sad-looking
L. quick tempered

Answer: 1-G, 2-B, 3-F, 4-A, 5-L, 6-H, 7-K, 8-E, 9-J, 10-D, 11-C, 12-I

Go the Extra Mile!

A *long face* describes a person who looks sad. Can you make up five more face idioms? For example, maybe someone with a *sharp face* looks mad. Be sure to include definitions for your five made-up idioms.

16

The Long Arm of the Law

by Megan Duhamel
illustrated by Doug Jones

JAIL

■ SCHOLASTIC

Learning Box

To bury one's head in the sand means to hide from danger. The phrase is based on an old-time belief that ostriches bury their heads in the sand. Turns out, that's a myth. But it's still a great idiom!

It looks like a showdown. Pa prepares for a stand.
The rest of us **bury our heads in the sand**.

14

Welcome to Dry Gulch

INN

Learning Box

Idioms are well-known phrases that mean something different from what the words actually say. Idioms use lively and colorful language to conjure up images in the reader's mind. For that reason, they are remembered and often passed down from generation to generation. *Tongue-in-cheek* and *behind someone's back* are two popular human-body idioms. Read on to learn 12 more!

Welcome to Dry Gulch, a Wild West town.
Come meet the people. I'll show you around.

3

Designed by Grafica, Inc.
ISBN-13: 978-0-545-13480-4 • ISBN-10: 0-545-13480-3
Copyright © 2009 by Lefty's Editorial Services.
All rights reserved. Printed in China
SCHOLASTIC and associated logos are trademarks and/or registered trademarks of Scholastic Inc.

First printing, September 2009

12 11 10 9 8 7 6 5 4 3 2 1   9 10 11 12 13 14/0

A

Learning Box

Green thumb is an idiom that means good at making plants grow. How did the phrase come to be? Folks that spend a lot of time gardening often get chlorophyll (the pigment of plants) on their hands, which can lead to green thumbs.

He just brought us flowers! He wants to be our chum.
The guy isn't a villain. He's just got a **green thumb**!

⑮

Learning Box

To *stay on one's toes* means to be alert. After all, it takes attention and concentration to maintain that challenging pose. Here's an idiom with the opposite meaning: *get caught flat-footed.*

There's Bee, the best roper that anyone knows.
She's great with a lasso. She **stays on her toes**.

④

B

Learning Box

A *chip on your shoulder* is an idiom that means you're ready to fight. In the early 1800s, there was a game in which one boy would dare another to knock a chip of wood off his shoulder. Knocking off the chip was guaranteed to start a fight.

Yikes! Who is that stranger in the tall hat of black?
There's a **chip on his shoulder**, and what's behind his back?

⑬

Learning Box

Wet behind the ears means young and inexperienced. This idiom is based on baby calves and colts. When these animals are first born, they are wet behind their ears.

I'll take over as the sheriff one of these years.
Right now, I'm too young and still **wet behind the ears**.

Learning Box

Hothead is an idiom used to describe a person with a quick temper. Think about it: When you get really mad, doesn't it feel like your head is heating up?

That cranky card player is called Quick-Draw Fred.
He gets mad when he loses 'cause he's a **hothead**.

Learning Box

This idiom means to say the wrong thing. If you told your friend, "I think pugs are ugly dogs," and it turns out he just got one for his birthday, that would be a perfect example of *putting your foot in your mouth*. What do saying the wrong thing and putting a foot in your mouth have in common? Both are very uncomfortable positions to be in!

Wyatt Blurt's hurtful words are remembered for weeks.
He **puts his foot in his mouth** whenever he speaks.

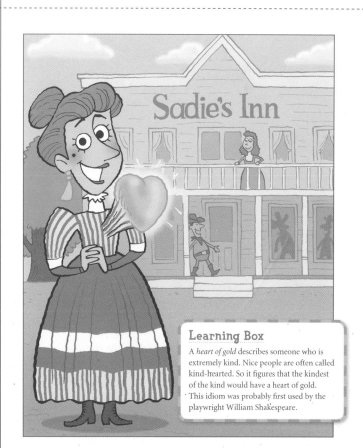

Learning Box

A *heart of gold* describes someone who is extremely kind. Nice people are often called kind-hearted. So it figures that the kindest of the kind would have a heart of gold. This idiom was probably first used by the playwright William Shakespeare.

Sadie Dupree has a huge **heart of gold**.
Her inn is the best in the West, I am told.

Learning Box

Butterfingers is an idiom used to describe people who are clumsy with their hands. Imagine that your fingers were made of slippery butter. You'd probably drop a lot of things, too!

Benny Beans plays the banjo at Sweeney's Saloon.
But those **butterfingers** won't let him finish a tune!

6

C

Learning Box

Long arm of the law is an idiom used to describe sheriffs and police officers. Why? Because no matter how far a bad guy runs, these lawmen usually catch him. It's almost as if they have a long arm.

Here's Sheriff McShane, the **long arm of the law**.
He's a very brave man, and he's also my pa.

11

Learning Box

A *long face* is used to describe someone who looks very sad. Why? Frowning tends to pull down people's chins, which makes them appear to have long faces. This idiom, like many others, relies on exaggeration to create a cartoony picture in the reader's mind.

Bart Blaine, the blacksmith, works at his own pace.
He's one gloomy guy with a very **long face**.

8

D

Learning Box

Joined at the hip refers to two people who are super-close. This idiom is based on conjoined twins, a pair of people whose bodies are actually joined together.

There are two cheerful cowgirls named Pattie and Pip.
They work as a team. They are **joined at the hip**.

9

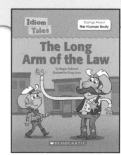

Dry Gulch Is Bone-Dry!

Dry Gulch needs more flowers. Lend them a hand—or just a green thumb!

One word is mixed up in each idiom below. Unscramble the letters to spell the word. Then write the word in the boxes, one letter in each square.

1. stay on your etso

2. put your ofot in your mouth

3. the long mra of the law

4. long ecfa

5. ehrta of gold

6. rbyu your head in the sand

7. chip on your oedurslh

8. wet behind the srae

In the boxes below, write the circled letters in order. Then read the message to see what the people of Dry Gulch have to say about flowers!

They're a sight for

!

Hint!
The answer is another human body idiom! Can you guess what it means?

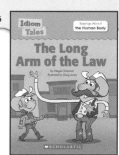

Stretch Your Mind!

Give your brain a workout by matching body idioms with their definitions.

Read each idiom on the left. Then read the definitions on the right. On the line next to each idiom, write the letter of the definition that matches. If you solve the puzzle correctly, you'll see a secret password down the side of the page.

_____ **1.** keep your chin up

_____ **2.** all thumbs

_____ **3.** twist someone's arm

_____ **4.** costs an arm and a leg

_____ **5.** have egg on your face

_____ **6.** let your hair down

L. This means to embarrass yourself. When you're a sloppy eater, food can get all over you. If it wound up here, you would hardly look your best!

E. This means to relax and be free. Why? It was once improper for women to do what the idiom describes in public. They kept their style in place with pins, and only took them out at home.

M. This means to stay cheerful when things go wrong. That's because when you're sad, your head droops. If you try to do the opposite, you might feel better!

C. This means something is very expensive. Why? Because it would take a whole lot of money to get anybody to sell these two very important things!

U. This means to be clumsy. It's easy to see why—imagine trying to use your hands if they were made this way!

S. This means to convince someone to do something. If you actually did what the idiom describes, it wouldn't feel very good. The person might agree with you just to get you to stop.

Hint!
It can help you bend over backwards or stay on your toes!

26

Idiom Match

On a separate sheet of paper, match each idiom with its meaning.

1. bolt out of the blue
2. chasing rainbows
3. once in a blue moon
4. don't have the foggiest
5. every cloud has a silver lining
6. dry spell
7. dancing up a storm
8. rain on someone's parade
9. blow everyone away
10. chill out
11. steal someone's thunder
12. made in the shade

A. using a lot of energy to dance
B. spoil a person's pleasure or plans
C. sudden and unexpected
D. relax
E. take attention away from someone
F. confused and having no idea
G. in an ideal situation
H. trying to achieve something that's unrealistic
I. a long period without success
J. easily defeat the competition
K. there is good in a bad situation
L. very rarely

Go the Extra Mile!

Create a weather idiom diary. Come up with at least five entries using idioms from this book. Here's an example: *I finished all my school work early. Now I get to just chill out.*

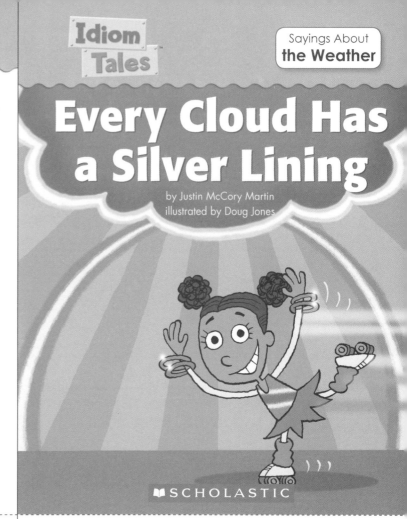

Every Cloud Has a Silver Lining

by Justin McCory Martin
illustrated by Doug Jones

SCHOLASTIC

Learning Box

When you *don't have the foggiest*, you have absolutely no idea. This is another idiom that paints a vivid picture. Think about a time you were very confused. Didn't it feel like your head was inside an incredibly thick fog?

I have to admit, Amber was totally awesome. Now, it's my turn. How can I possibly compete with her act? I **don't have the foggiest**. Still, I'll give it try. Here goes . . .

Learning Box

Idioms are well-known phrases that mean something different from what the words actually say. Idioms use lively and colorful language to conjure up images in the reader's mind. For that reason, they are remembered and often passed down from generation to generation. *Fair-weather friend* and *it's raining cats and dogs* are two popular weather idioms. Read on to learn 12 more!

Hi there, I'm Darla B. Dazzle. The big school talent show is about to begin and I'm super-excited. This year I'm going to roller-skate while I sing. I'd like to see someone top that!

Designed by Grafica, Inc.
ISBN-13: 978-0-545-13478-1 • ISBN-10: 0-545-13478-1
Copyright © 2009 by Lefty's Editorial Services.
All rights reserved. Printed in China.
SCHOLASTIC and associated logos are trademarks and/or registered trademarks of Scholastic Inc.

First printing, September 2009

12 11 10 9 8 7 6 5 4 3 2 1   9 10 11 12 13 14/0

Learning Box

Every cloud has a silver lining means there's good in bad situations. The idiom was used by the famous 17th century English poet John Milton. He described sunlight shining through a dark stormy cloud. It made the cloud look beautiful, like it had a silver lining.

Well, as you may have guessed, Amber won the talent show. But **every cloud has a silver lining**. She just asked me to perform with her next year! Think about it: The two of us roller-skating AND singing AND juggling. I'd like to see someone top that!

Learning Box

Chasing rainbows means trying to achieve something that's unrealistic, even impossible. You've probably heard stories about pots of gold at the end of rainbows. Of course, these are just stories. Someone who chases rainbows hoping to find gold would definitely be attempting the impossible.

The first act is a gymnast named Polly Prattle. She's walking on her hands. Wow, that's pretty impressive! But Polly is **chasing rainbows** if she thinks she can beat me.

Learning Box

To steal someone's thunder means to do something to take attention away from him or her. In 1704, John Dennis invented a new method for creating the sound of thunder, which he used in his play called *Appius and Virginia*. After the play failed, the same sound effect was copied in a production of *Macbeth*. This caused Dennis to angrily remark, "They will not let my play run, but they will steal my thunder."

BOOM!

I can't believe it! She is roller-skating AND singing AND juggling. Egads! Amber has **stolen my thunder**!

Wait, another act has just been announced. It's the new girl in my class—Amber Appleton. Wow, this is a **bolt out of the blue**! I wonder what she is going to do.

12

I'm feeling good. I'm not even a tiny bit nervous. I'll just **chill out** until it's my turn.

5

Check out Colin Chen. He's **dancing up a storm**. His is the best act yet, but he still can't compete with the one and only Darla B. Dazzle.

10

I'm feeling great! No one in this show can possibly have a better act than mine. I have it **made in the shade**.

7

Here comes the second act. It's the Thompson triplets' marching band. I don't mean **to rain on their parade**, but they don't stand a chance against yours truly.

C

I'm feeling pretty fantastic! Let me up on that stage. I'm going to **blow everyone away**.

Look who's on stage now. Gabby Gates plays the violin every year. She's not bad, but she never wins. And with me on the scene, I don't think she'll break her **dry spell** today.

D

I'm feeling fantastic! C'mon, tell the truth. How often does someone have an act as special as mine? Maybe **once in a blue moon**?

Darla the Superstar

Help Darla B. Dazzle and Amber Appleton shine in their new act!

Choose an idiom from the box to complete each sentence below.

chasing
rainbows

made in
the shade

once in a
blue moon

every cloud has
a silver lining

bolt out of
the blue

dancing up
a storm

dry spell

don't have
the foggiest

1. When Darla and Amber started putting on shows, they drew a huge crowd for every performance. They thought they had it _____.

2. But after a while, people got tired of the act and stopped buying tickets. Darla and Amber had to find a way to break their _____.

3. "We already roller-skate, sing, and juggle," said Amber. "What else could we possibly fit into the act? I _____ _____."

4. Darla couldn't think of anything either. But then an idea came to her like a _____. "We can teach my dog to skate and put him in the act!" she said.

5. Amber thought it couldn't work. "Your dog will never learn to skate," she said. "Stop _____."

6. Darla's dog didn't learn to roller skate, after all. But _____, because he learned to do something just as amazing!

7. As Amber and Darla practiced their songs, Darla's dog started moving to the beat. Before long, he was _____ _____!

8. So if you want to see a great act, get a ticket to Darla and Amber's show. But hurry—something this good comes along only _____!

Stormy Weather

Solve this word search and things will clear up!

Read the words in the box from top to bottom. Have you ever heard this weather idiom? Find and circle each word in the puzzle. Words can go across, down, or on a diagonal.

LIGHTNING
NEVER
STRIKES
TWICE

```
              A N T
N I M S T R I K E S P W R
  E L I G H T N I N G I
  V O B A B L E E V C
  E N E T W O N T H A E
  P P E N R A G
      A I N
```

Now get the message loud and clear! Write the uncircled letters in order (going across, from top to bottom) on the blanks below. Then read the words to see the idiom's meaning!

— — — — — — — — — — —

— ,

— — — ' — — — — — — — — — —

Idiom Match

On a separate sheet of paper, match each idiom with its meaning.

1. yellow-bellied
2. true colors
3. blue
4. green
5. green around the gills
6. red flag
7. purple with rage
8. good as gold

A. sad
B. sick
C. cowardly
D. warning sign
E. super angry
F. honest
G. inexperienced
H. extremely good

Go the Extra Mile!

There are tons of color idioms. Here are ten more: *local color, red herring, green-eyed monster, blue streak, pink slip, silver tongue, golden opportunity, white lie, gray matter, black sheep*. Find out the meaning of each idiom. Then turn on your imagination and use them to write a wacky tale!

True Colors

by Justin McCory Martin
illustrated by Doug Jones

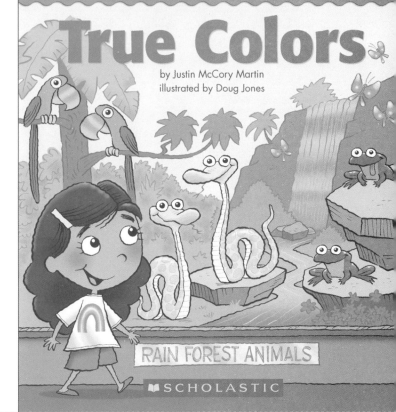

RAIN FOREST ANIMALS

■ SCHOLASTIC

Learning Box

A *red-letter day* is a happy, important, or memorable day. This idiom is from medieval times, when important dates such as festivals were written on calendars in red letters.

So he moved them all back without further delay.
And for every last one, it was a **red-letter day**!

Learning Box

Idioms are well-known phrases that mean something different from what the words actually say. Idioms use lively and colorful language to conjure up images in the reader's mind. For that reason, they are remembered and often passed down from generation to generation. *Paint the town red* and *talk a blue streak* are two popular color idioms. Read on to learn 12 more!

Here's the colorful tale of my trip to the zoo.
I think you'll enjoy it. I certainly do.

Designed by Grafica, Inc.
ISBN-13: 978-0-545-22413-0 • ISBN-10: 0-545-22413-6
Copyright © 2009 by Lefty's Editorial Services.
All rights reserved. Printed in China
SCHOLASTIC and associated logos are trademarks and/or registered trademarks of Scholastic Inc.

12 11 10 9 8 7 6 5 4 3 2 1   10 11 12 13 14/0

A

Learning Box

True colors is an idiom used when something is honest. It is from the 1700s and is based on an idiom that means the opposite. A ship was *flying false colors* if it was using the wrong flag to try to trick other ships.

At last, life was normal again at the zoo.
The animals' **true colors** were all shining through!

15

Learning Box

Blue is an idiom that means sad. You can look, feel, or be blue. You can also *get the blues.* Other blue idioms include *blue in the face,* which means angry to the point of frustration, and *out of the blue,* which means without warning.

In with the penguins, I noticed a gnu.
She did not belong there. She **looked really blue**.

4

B

Learning Box

Good as gold describes someone or something that's extremely good. After all, what's more precious and valuable than gold? This is another idiom that has been around a long time because of its alliteration. "Good as gold" is a lot more fun to say than "good as diamonds."

"I mixed up the creatures. They like that, I'm told."
"Unmix them," I said. "Then they'll be **good as gold**."

13

Learning Box

Green means immature or inexperienced. This idiom is based on how a young plant looks before it has flowers or fruit. It is simply green.

So I ran to the zookeeper but, boy, **was he green**.
"I made changes!" he boasted, "Haven't you seen?"

Learning Box

If something gives you *gray hair* that means it causes stress. This idiom is based on the notion that extreme worry can cause your hair to turn gray. Scientists are not sure if there's any truth to this idea, but it sure makes for a colorful idiom. It dates to the early 1600s.

A polar bear paced in the rain forest room.
He was **getting gray hair**. He felt nothing but gloom.

Learning Box

White as a sheet means shocked and scared. This idiom is based on the notion that people turn pale when frightened. And nothing is whiter than a clean sheet, right?

Rooming with rodents gave the elephant a fright.
He was **white as a sheet**. What a terrible sight!

Learning Box

Yellow-bellied is an idiom that means cowardly. Going back to ancient times, the color yellow has been used to describe people with weak character. Meanwhile, the belly is a very vulnerable spot on the body. This idiom is a double-whammy. Someone with a yellow belly would be very weak and fearful indeed.

Some toucans were perched in the tiger's tall tree.
They were all **yellow-bellied**. Hey, wouldn't you be?

At the seal tank, I saw a giraffe with a ball.
Another **red flag**. This was not right at all!

6

C

I walked past two crocs with **black looks** on their faces.
Good grief! All of the animals were in the wrong places!

11

The boa as well had been moved from his cage.
And his new habitat made him **purple with rage**.

8

D

Meanwhile, the flamingos were **green around the gills**—
'Cause a monkey's bananas got caught in their bills.

9

Color Confusion

The zookeeper is all mixed up again! Help him unscramble his idioms.

One word is mixed up in each idiom below. Unscramble the letters to spell the word. Then write the word in the boxes, one letter in each square.

1. feeling eblu

2. good as gldo

3. rplepu with rage

4. ollyew bellied

5. true osrloc

6. ewthi as a sheet

7. erneg around the gills

8. edr-letter day

9. ygra hair

10. kbcla look

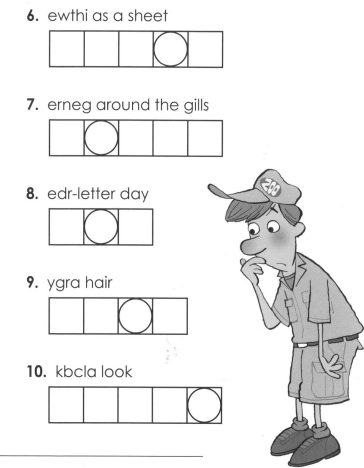

In the boxes below, write the circled letters in order. Then read the message to answer the riddle!

Question: Why didn't the toucans like living with the parrots?
Answer: Because they talked a

 !

Hint!
The answer is another color idiom! Can you guess what it means?

The Color Code

Crack the code by matching color idioms with their definitions.

Read each idiom on the left. Then read the definitions on the right. On the line next to each idiom, write the letter of the definition that matches. If you solve the puzzle correctly, you'll see a secret password down the side of the page.

_____ **1.** give the green light

_____ **2.** black and blue

_____ **3.** like white on rice

_____ **4.** red-eye flight

_____ **5.** roll out the red carpet

_____ **6.** blackout

_____ **7.** wave the white flag

Y. This idiom refers to a late-night or overnight plane trip. It's hard to sleep on a plane—the expression describes how you might look when you land!

A. This means to stick to someone or something very closely. That's because it's impossible to separate this food from its color!

C. This means to give permission for something to happen or move forward. Why? The color means "Go" on a traffic signal.

S. This means to give up, or surrender. It's a symbol that armies use to show that they have lost a battle.

N. This idiom refers to what happens when electricity is lost. That's because everything looks this color when all the lights go out!

R. This idiom refers to having a bruise. It's easy to see why—the mark a bruise makes on your skin is usually these two colors.

O. This means to give someone royal or special treatment. The idiom comes from a traditional color of floor covering used for visiting kings and queens. Today, it's used for movie stars.

Hint!
These can help you show your true colors!

38

Idiom Match

On a separate sheet of paper, match each idiom with its meaning.

1. in stitches
2. under the weather
3. dog-tired
4. tickled pink
5. on cloud nine
6. pleased as punch
7. over the moon
8. down in the dumps
9. happy as a clam

10. ants in your pants
11. green with envy
12. bent out of shape

A. content as a clam
B. laughing very hard
C. not feeling well
D. very pleased
E. frustrated and annoyed
F. extremely restless
G. so delighted you turn pink
H. very jealous
I. so overjoyed you feel like you could rocket into space
J. exhausted
K. sad or depressed
L. so blissfully happy it feels like you're floating on a cloud

ANSWERS: 1.B 2.C 3.J 4.G 5.L 6.D 7.I 8.K 9.A 10.F 11.H 12.E

Go the Extra Mile!

A lot of idioms describe different kinds of happiness including *tickled pink*, *on cloud nine*, and *over the moon*. Can you think of more? Make a list of other well-known happiness idioms and/or come up with some of your own!

Idiom Tales

Over the Moon

by Justin McCory Martin
illustrated by Kelly Kennedy

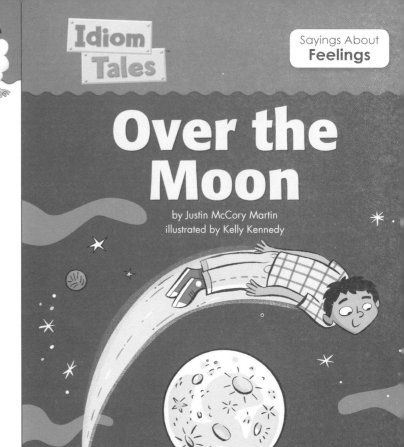

SCHOLASTIC

Learning Box

Dog-tired means exhausted. Here's how it came about: Alfred the Great was king of England a long time ago. Each day, he'd ask his two sons to chase his pet dogs. The boy who caught the most dogs got to sit closest to King Alfred at dinner. Both boys wound up *dog-tired*.

Then Matt does a bit of shopping with Sue.
The mall makes him joyful but **dog-tired**, too.

Learning Box

Idioms are well-known phrases that mean something different from what the words actually say. Idioms use lively and colorful language to conjure up images in the reader's mind. For that reason, they are remembered and often passed down from generation to generation. *Seeing red* and *weak in the knees* are two popular emotion idioms. Read on to learn 12 more!

Who is this? It's Matt McKay!
Let's see how he's feeling today.

Designed by Grafica, Inc.
ISBN-13: 978-0-545-13479-8 • ISBN-10: 0-545-13479-X
Copyright © 2009 by Lefty's Editorial Services.
All rights reserved. Printed in China
SCHOLASTIC and associated logos are trademarks and/or registered trademarks of Scholastic Inc.

First printing, September 2009

12 11 10 9 8 7 6 5 4 3 2 1   9 10 11 12 13 14/0

A

Learning Box

Happy as a clam is an idiom used to describe great contentment. This phrase actually comes from a longer phrase, *happy as a clam at high tide*. Why are clams so happy at high tide? Because then they are underwater and there are no predators to gobble them up!

When it's finally bedtime, what does Matt say?
"I'm **happy as a clam**. It's been quite a day!"

15

Learning Box

Under the weather means you are not feeling well. In the old days, a lot of people traveled by boat. When the weather was bad, some became seasick and were sent below deck to recover. Thus, they were said to be "under the weather."

When Matt wakes up, the world looks bleak.
He's under the weather. It's been a tough week.

4

B

Learning Box

Pleased as punch is a phrase used to describe extreme pleasure. It comes from an old-time puppet show called *Punch and Judy*, in which a character named Punch is always very pleased with himself. But the meaning of phrases change over time. Nowadays, no one can remember that old puppet show. When people hear "pleased as punch" they think of a delicious pitcher of punch and how pleasing that would be.

After that, it's time for swimming and sun.
Matt's **pleased as punch**. Wow, this is fun!

13

Learning Box

Green with envy means very jealous. This idiom originated in America. At first, it was just used to describe people who were envious of those with more money. Paper money IS green, after all!

At the rink, a girl is zooming so fast—
Matt's **green with envy** as she speeds past!

12

Learning Box

Over the moon is an idiom that means overjoyed. It comes from the 16th century nursery rhyme "Hey, Diddle, Diddle" in which a joyful cow jumps over the moon.

Then Matt remembers it's Saturday—Yay!
He's **over the moon**. He's got all day to play.

5

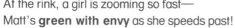

Learning Box

Down in the dumps means sad or depressed. This very old idiom probably originated in Germany.

Next, Matt shoots some hoops. He dribbles and jumps.
But when the ball gets stuck, he's **down in the dumps**.

10

Learning Box

On cloud nine means blissfully happy. Similar idioms about being happy include *walking on air* and *on top of the world*.

Matt eats a big breakfast—eggs, taters, and ham.
He's **on cloud nine**. Pass the biscuits and jam!

7

Learning Box

Ants in your pants is an idiom used to express extreme restlessness. If you had ants crawling up and down your legs, would you be able to stand still? No way!

So much to do! Matt feels lots of stress.
He has **ants in his pants** as he hurries to dress.

6

C

Learning Box

Tickled pink means delighted. Why? People tend to turn pink when they are tickled.

"Hey, buddy," says Steve. "Let's go to the rink."
Skating's the best, so Matt's **tickled pink**.

11

Learning Box

In stitches is an idiom to describe something so funny that it splits your side and requires stitches. This phrase was first used by William Shakespeare, in *Twelfth Night*, a play he wrote in 1601.

Matt plops on the couch to watch "Dinky Ditches."
The cartoon's so funny, it has him **in stitches**.

8

D

Learning Box

Bent out of shape means frustrated and annoyed. Think about it: If you were literally bent out of shape, you'd be quite uncomfortable AND unhappy.

Matt gets **bent out of shape** when he looks at his bike.
Both tires are flat. It's as low as a trike!

9

Don't Be Cross!

Help Matt McKay get back on cloud nine by solving this crossword.

Choose a word from the box to complete each sentence correctly. Then write your answers in the crossword puzzle.

tired

pleased

over

happy

down

tickled

bent

under

envy

Across

2. Someone who's sad and depressed is _____ in the dumps.

4. Someone who's frustrated and annoyed is _____ out of shape.

8. Someone who's very jealous is green with_____.

9. Someone who's experiencing extreme enjoyment or pleasure is _____ as punch.

Down

1. Someone who's not feeling well is _____ the weather.

3. Someone who's absolutely delighted is _____ pink.

5. Someone who's exhausted is dog-_____ .

6. Someone who is full of joy is _____ the moon.

7. Someone who's very content is _____ as a clam.

Moody Matt McKay

Crack the code and help Matt find new idioms to describe his feelings.

There are two definitions for the underlined idiom in each sentence below, but only one is correct! Read the sentence. Then circle the letter next to the correct answer.

1. Matt, Steve, and Sue had plans to go on a picnic. Matt was so
   excited that he was <u>on the edge of his seat</u> waiting for the day to arrive.
   - **B.** feeling that he had no comfortable furniture
   - **C.** feeling suspense and expectation

2. But it rained all day, so they had to stay indoors. "There's nothing to do!" said Matt.
   "I'm going <u>stir-crazy</u>!"
   - **D.** feeling trapped and extremely restless
   - **E.** feeling foolish for moving around too much

3. Steve suggested they watch a movie. "That's a great idea!" said Matt.
   "A good movie would make me <u>fit as a fiddle</u>."
   - **E.** feeling very well; in good health
   - **F.** feeling out of place; feeling you don't fit in

4. Matt was afraid to watch the thriller that Sue suggested, but he was
   embarrassed to say so. He felt <u>tongue-tied</u>.
   - **M.** twisting information in order to trick someone
   - **N.** unable to express yourself, often from shyness

5. But Steve wanted to watch a comedy, which made Matt feel much
   better. "That <u>takes a load off my mind</u>!" he thought.
   - **O.** gives a feeling of relief; stops from worrying
   - **P.** makes dizzy and lightheaded

6. Matt had a great time watching movies and laughing with his friends. "I thought the rain
   would ruin my whole weekend," he told them, "but you two really <u>made my day</u>!"
   - **R.** felt forced into doing something
   - **S.** gave a feeling of great pleasure and satisfaction

Now crack the code! Each number below stands for one of the questions. Write the letter of your answer above the number. Then read the message to see why Matt's feelings keep changing!

He's always having

$\overline{}$ $\overline{}$ $\overline{}$ $\overline{}$ $\overline{}$ $\overline{}$ **thoughts!**
 6   3   1   5   4   2

Hint!

The answer is another feelings idiom! Can you guess what it means?

Idiom Match

On a separate sheet of paper, match each idiom with its meaning.

1. couch potato
2. in a pickle
3. nice as pie
4. smart cookie
5. tough nut to crack
6. go bananas
7. the big cheese
8. full of beans
9. cool as a cucumber
10. apple of everyone's eye
11. peas in a pod
12. packed in like sardines

A. friendly and kind
B. very important person
C. act wild and wacky
D. in a very crowded place
E. calm
F. silly and full of energy
G. in big trouble
H. a person who is greatly loved
I. someone who likes to lie around
J. very intelligent
K. a person who is hard to figure out
L. people who are close and have something in common

Answers: 1.I 2.G 3.A 4.J 5.K 6.C 7.B 8.F 9.E 10.H 11.L 12.D

Go the Extra Mile!

Use food idioms to describe characters in your favorite books, movies, and television shows. For example, Snow White is as *nice as pie* and the Gingerbread Boy is *full of beans*. Make sure to explain your thinking.

16

Sayings About **Food**

Peas in a Pod

by Xander Davies
illustrated by Kelly Kennedy

SCHOLASTIC

Learning Box

Nice as pie is an idiom used to describe someone who is friendly and kind. Other pie-related sayings include *easy as pie* (very easy) and *apple pie order* (well organized).

My marvelous mom is last but not least.
She's **nice as pie.** She's fixing a feast!

14

Learning Box

Idioms are well-known phrases that mean something different from what the words actually say. Idioms use colorful and lively language to conjure up images in the reader's mind. For that reason, they are remembered and often passed down from generation to generation. *Piece of cake* and *good egg* are two popular food idioms. Read on to learn 12 more!

Come meet the family! My name is Pat.
I have three sisters, four brothers, a mom, dad, and cat.

3

Designed by Grafica, Inc.
ISBN-13: 978-0-545-13481-1 • ISBN-10: 0-545-13481-1
Copyright © 2009 by Lefty's Editorial Services.
All rights reserved. Printed in China
SCHOLASTIC and associated logos are trademarks and/or registered trademarks of Scholastic Inc.

First printing, September 2009

12 11 10 9 8 7 6 5 4 3 2 1   9 10 11 12 13 14/0

A

Learning Box

Peas in a pod describes people who are close and have something in common, like the members of a family. The phrase dates back to the 1500s, when people spent a lot of time preparing vegetables for meals and noticed the similarity among all the peas in a single pod.

Our home sure is crowded, all night and all day.
We're **peas in a pod**—and we like it that way!

15

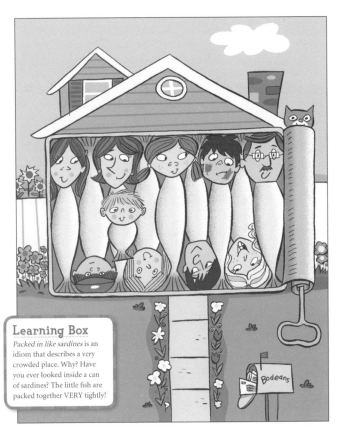

Learning Box

Packed in like sardines is an idiom that describes a very crowded place. Why? Have you ever looked inside a can of sardines? The little fish are packed together VERY tightly!

Our clan is quite awesome! We're called the Bodeans.
But our house is so small, we're **packed in like sardines**.

4

B

Learning Box

The big cheese is an idiom that describes a very important person. Long ago, the word *cheese* was slang for something that was worth paying attention to. Thus, folks began using the term *big cheese* to refer to an individual they considered extra important.

Here's Dad, **the big cheese**, in his basement workshop.
He's building a birdhouse. That's pretty cool, Pop!

13

Learning Box

Go bananas is an idiom that means to act wild and wacky. What animal really loves bananas? Monkeys! And how do they behave? Wild and wacky!

Mittens, the cat, loves to race through the house.
She really **goes bananas** when she sees a mouse.

12

Learning Box

A *smart cookie* is someone that is very intelligent. Another cookie-related idiom is *tough cookie*. It is used to describe a person who is brave and determined.

This is Cindy, the oldest. She's so super-cool.
She's such a **smart cookie**. She does great in school!

5

Learning Box

In a pickle means in big trouble. Think about it: Would you like to be stuck in a jar full of stinky vinegar, like a pickle? No way! That would present a big problem. The idiom was first used in the 1500s by the Dutch.

Nelly is naughty. She loves sneaking snacks.
Now she's **in a pickle** 'cause she left behind tracks!

10

Learning Box

Tough nut to crack is an idiom that means that someone or something is hard to figure out. Ever use a nutcracker? Some nuts are simply tough to crack. This idiom dates to the 1700s and was even uttered by Ben Franklin.

The quietest kid is my brother named Zack.
He's a bit of a mystery—a **tough nut to crack**.

7

Learning Box

Cool as a cucumber is an idiom used to describe someone who is calm. The idiom was first used in the 1500s, when people noticed that the inside of a cucumber is much cooler than the outside air.

Here's big brother Billy. He never gets stressed.
He's **cool as a cucumber**. I'm always impressed.

C

Learning Box

The *apple of everyone's eye* is an idiom used to describe someone who is greatly loved. Here's why: The dark circle in the center of your eye is called the pupil. In ancient times, people thought that the pupil was shaped like an apple. Thus, someone who's the *apple of your eye* is the center, the most important.

This is Bobby, the baby. He's totally shy.
Still, he's the **apple of everyone's eye**.

Learning Box

Full of beans means filled with energy, especially silly energy. It's a very old idiom, first used to describe horses. Back then, someone noticed that horses that were fed beans became very lively.

Meet Suzy, the silliest of all the Bodeans.
She makes everyone chuckle. She's so **full of beans!**

D

Learning Box

Couch potato is an idiom that describes someone who lies around and barely moves. The idiom was first used in the 1970s, when televisions were becoming more popular. Think about it: Someone who lies around watching TV—or playing video games—might appear lumpy and motionless, like a potato.

Rick likes to relax. He's a total **couch potato**.
His room always looks like it was hit by a tornado!

Who Is Pat Bodean?

In *Peas in a Pod*, Pat describes each Bodean—except herself! Help fix the mix-up.

One word is mixed up in each idiom below. Unscramble the letters to spell the word. Then write the word in the boxes, one letter in each square.

1. tough utn to crack

2. go nabaasn

3. in a kcpiel

4. nice as iep

5. packed in like rsiedans

6. couch opoatt

7. the big ceehes

8. lpepa of everyone's eye

9. cool as a urumeccb

10. aesp in a pod

11. smart okceio

12. full of sbnae

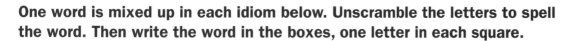

In the boxes below, write the circled letters in order. Then read the message to see how the Bodean family feels about Pat!

Hint!
The answer is another food idiom! Can you guess what it means?

They think she

A Milky Mystery

Don't cry over this tear-shaped puzzle—find the food idiom instead!

Read the words in the box in order. Have you ever heard this food idiom? Find and circle each word in the puzzle. Words can go across, down, or on a diagonal.

THERE

IS

NO

USE

CRYING

OVER

SPILLED

MILK

Now solve the mystery! Write the uncircled letters in order (going across, top to bottom) on the blanks below. Then read the message to see the idiom's meaning!

___ __ __ ____ ____

_____ ____ _____

Idiom Match

On a separate sheet of paper, match each idiom with its meaning.

1. dressed to the nines
2. goody-two-shoes
3. earn your stripes
4. buckle down
5. ace up your sleeve
6. shaking in your boots
7. bee in your bonnet
8. eat your hat

A. obsessed by an idea
B. to have a secret advantage
C. wearing fashionable clothes
D. to be incredibly surprised
E. show you have the skills
F. someone who tries to act perfect
G. to work seriously
H. to be very nervous or scared

Answer: 1C 2F 3E 4G 5B 6H 7A 8D

Go the Extra Mile!

Some of the most memorable idioms make use of alliteration or rhyme such as *bee in your bonnet* or *ants in your pants*. Why? Poetic language makes phrases stick in a person's mind. Dream up five to ten new clothing idioms that use alliteration or rhyme such as *tough as trousers* or a *mouse in your blouse*. Be sure to provide your definitions, too.

Shaking in My Boots

by Tess Montague
illustrated by Kelly Kennedy

■ SCHOLASTIC

Learning Box

To *eat your hat* means to be incredibly surprised. After all, eating a hat would be a surprising and unexpected thing to do. This is a popular English-language idiom used by writers such as Charles Dickens.

HJÄLP
AIDE
HELP SAIDIA
AYUDA

A few hours later, we were in luck. A plane was buzzing overhead and all the commotion caught the pilot's eye.

"Look!" shouted my father.

"We're saved!" screamed Winnifred.

"Well, I'll **eat my hat**!" I exclaimed.

Learning Box

Idioms are well-known phrases that mean something different from what the words actually say. Idioms use lively and colorful language to conjure up images in the reader's mind. For that reason, they are remembered and often passed down from generation to generation. *Rags to riches* and *button your lip* are two popular clothing idioms. Read on to learn 12 more!

Hi there! I'm Kevin Caruso and I'm in the fifth grade. Want to know what I did on my summer vacation? I got stranded on a desert island.

Designed by Grafica, Inc.
ISBN-13: 978-0-545-22412-3 • ISBN-10: 0-545-22412-8
Copyright © 2009 by Lefty's Editorial Services.
All rights reserved. Printed in China
SCHOLASTIC and associated logos are trademarks and/or registered trademarks of Scholastic Inc.

12 11 10 9 8 7 6 5 4 3 2 1   10 11 12 13 14/0

A

Learning Box

To *earn your stripes* means that you have shown you have skills and can accomplish an important task. This idiom is based on a military custom, where skillful soldiers earn stripes to wear on their uniforms.

The pilot landed her plane on the island and rescued us.
"Way to work together," said my dad. "You really **earned your stripes**!"
And that's what I did on my summer vacation. What did you do?

 15

Learning Box

To be *too big for your britches* means to act conceited or to have an inflated sense of self-worth. This is an American idiom that dates back more than 200 years. *Britches* is old-fashioned slang for *pants*.

I may be young, but I'm a darn good sailor. Think I'm acting **too big for my britches**? Well, I'm not. The Captain says I'm the best first mate he ever had. And he should know—he's my dad.

4

B

Learning Box

If you have *a bee in your bonnet* it means you've been struck by an idea and are obsessed. The idiom first appeared in "Mad Maid's Song," a 1648 English poem by Robert Herrick. It's a vivid idiom: Isn't having an idea you can't shake kind of like having a bee buzzing in a bonnet?

Last but not least, it was Winnifred's turn. She had a **bee in her bonnet** about the best way to save the day. She and Winston climbed two trees and began waving palm leaves back and forth to attract attention. Pretty clever. I guess Winnifred wasn't so bad after all.

13

"My turn," announced Mrs. Puffington.

She rubbed two sticks together and made a gigantic bonfire. The smoke rose high into the air for all to see.

"Darling," said Mr. Puffington, "your survival skills really **knock my socks off**!"

12

Now, let's continue with my story. My dad and I were hired to take a group of people on a one-day cruise. The passengers included Mr. and Mrs. Puffington, their daughter, Winnifred, and her dog, Winston. I liked Winston immediately. Winnifred, however, seemed like a real **Goody-two-shoes**.

5

Dr. Beeber **put on his thinking cap**. He thought and thought. Then he got an idea. He took a stick and wrote "help" in giant letters in five different languages.

"Now people from different cultures will be able to help us," he said.

10

The voyage started well. Then a humongous storm hit. There was thunder and lightning. There were wild winds and giant waves. Needless to say, I was **shaking in my boots**.

7

Learning Box

To have an *ace up your sleeve* means that a person has an advantage, perhaps one that others don't know about. This is an idiom from the old Wild West, where cowboys played cards and often cheated. A cowboy with an ace up his sleeve had a secret advantage in a card game.

Learning Box

Dressed to the nines describes someone wearing fashionable and attention-grabbing clothing. This idiom became popular in the 1800s, but no one is certain of its origin. Maybe it's based on an Old English idiom *dressed to then eyne*, which means fashionable all the way up to your eyes (*eyne*).

The other two passengers were Dr. Beeber and Alexis Sparkle. Dr. Beeber was a brilliant professor. He spoke five languages. Alexis Sparkle was a glamorous actress. She arrived **dressed to the nines**.

C

6

Next, Alexis Sparkle stepped forward.

"I, too, have an **ace up my sleeve**," she said dramatically.

Alexis rummaged in her purse and pulled out a mirror. She held it up to the sun, making a bright flash that could be seen for one hundred miles!

11

Learning Box

Hanging by a thread means that someone is in an unsafe position. This idiom is based on a 2,400-year-old Greek story, *The Sword of Damocles*. Damocles prepares a feast for the king. But it's a trick. When the king looks up, there's a sword about to fall from the ceiling onto his head. The sword is *hanging by a thread*.

Long story short, our boat crashed on a desert island. We hollered and hollered for help. But there was no one to hear our cries. Tired and hungry, we were **hanging by a thread**.

D

8

Learning Box

Buckle down means to work seriously and hard. It's an old idiom based on knights buckling their suits of armor to prepare for serious combat.

It was a scary situation, but my dad took charge. He told us to **buckle down** and come up with a plan. To get off of the island, we'd need to work together.

9

Kevin Caruso's Cruise Line

Everybody deserves an exciting vacation! Help Kevin write the ad for his new tour.

Choose an idiom from the box to complete each sentence below.

shaking in your boots
eat my hat
put on your thinking cap
ace up your sleeve
bee in your bonnet
hanging by a thread
knock your socks off

1. Has it been a long time since you went on a trip? If you're bored with staying at home, you probably have a _____ to take a vacation.

2. There are lots of places to go, and it can be hard to pick just one. You really need to _____ _____ to decide what kind of trip you want to take.

3. Caruso Cruise Line has the answer! If you want excitement and adventure, the Desert Island Drama tour is guaranteed to _____!

4. Be a part of the action as we ride through rough waters with no land in sight. The chills you'll feel aboard this floating fright-fest will have you _____ _____!

5. But don't worry, because you'll have an _____ _____. You'll be sailing with an expert captain who knows the way to a safe island!

6. In the Desert Island Drama tour, we act out our real-life shipwreck—and rescue! You'll feel like your future is _____, but you'll be completely safe!

7. So if you want thrills, call Caruso Cruise Line and sign up for a tour today. If it's not the most exciting trip of your life, I'll _____!

Let's Play Dress-Up!

Win this game by matching clothing idioms with their definitions.

Read each idiom on the left. Then read the definitions on the right. On the line next to each idiom, write the letter of the definition that matches. If you solve the puzzle correctly, you'll see a secret password down the side of the page.

_____ **1.** take your hat off to someone

_____ **2.** wolf in sheep's clothing

_____ **3.** keep your shirt on

_____ **4.** tighten your belt

_____ **5.** fit like a glove

_____ **6.** feather in your cap

_____ **7.** deep pockets and short arms

S. This is used to tell somebody to calm down or be patient. Why? The item of clothing was once very expensive—someone getting ready to fight would take it off so it wouldn't get ruined!

M. This refers to a success you can be proud of. It's a tradition to add a plume to the headwear of a soldier who has been brave or successful in battle.

E. This describes a wealthy person who is stingy. Why? People carry money in these parts of their clothes, and roomy ones can hold the most. But if you can't reach in, you won't spend any of it!

C. This means you admire someone. It comes from the tradition of uncovering your head as a sign of respect.

O. This refers to a person who seems kind but is actually unkind. It probably comes from a fable about an animal that disguises itself to get closer to its prey.

T. This means to spend less money. Why? When people can't afford food, they lose weight, and their pants get loose. It's cheaper to do what the idiom describes than to buy new pants!

U. This means to suit someone perfectly. Why? The item of clothing is designed to match the shape of your hand, in order to cover it just right!

Hint!
This can help you get all dressed up!

56

Idiom Match

On a separate sheet of paper, match each idiom with its meaning.

1. clear another hurdle
2. behind the eight ball
3. down to the wire
4. bowled over
5. skate on thin ice
6. get into the swing
7. sail through
8. meet your match
9. drop the ball
10. get the hang of
11. kick off
12. slam dunk

A. take a foolish risk
B. stunned and amazed
C. easy task
D. get past something that's in your way
E. come across someone who is equally good at something
F. learn how to do something
G. running out of time
H. begin something
I. in a bad position
J. become comfortable with something
K. succeed quickly
L. make a mistake

Go the Extra Mile!

Here's the beginning of a story: *The door opened and a robot stepped through. Megan knew she had* <u>met her match</u>. Finish the story using at least five other sports idioms.

16

Slam Dunk!

by Justin McCory Martin
illustrated by Doug Jones

■ SCHOLASTIC

Learning Box

Down to the wire means running out of time. This idiom comes from horse racing. In the old days, a wire was used to mark the finish line. So if you are getting down to the wire, you don't have much time left to complete a task.

One more task. Ten more seconds. Go, Timmy, go! Get that pillow inside the pillowcase. Five more seconds. It's **down to the wire**. Hurry, Timmy, hurry!

14

Learning Box

Idioms are well-known phrases that mean something different from what the words actually say. Idioms use lively and colorful language to conjure up images in the reader's mind. For that reason, they are remembered and often passed down from generation to generation. *Play ball* and *win by a nose* are two popular sports idioms. Read on to learn 12 more!

Hello, fans. I'm Jake Jabber, announcer for All-Sports Television. Today, I will be bringing you an exciting live event. I will be doing a play-by-play as Timmy Talbot cleans his room.

3

Designed by Grafica, Inc.
ISBN-13: 978-0-545-13477-4 • ISBN-10: 0-545-13477-3
Copyright © 2009 by Lefty's Editorial Services.
All rights reserved. Printed in China
SCHOLASTIC and associated logos are trademarks and/or registered trademarks of Scholastic Inc.

First printing, September 2009

12 11 10 9 8 7 6 5 4 3 2 1   9 10 11 12 13 14/0

Learning Box

Bowled over means stunned and amazed. The idiom comes from bowling. Picture all those pins toppling over. Think about it: If someone did something incredible, you might feel like falling down, too!

Phew, he did it! Timmy's parents have just arrived. His room is so clean that they cannot believe it. They are **bowled over**. What a remarkable moment! I don't think anyone will ever forget this. I'm Jake Jabber, All-Sports Television. Tune in the same time next week for live lawn mowing.

Learning Box

Kicking off is an idiom that means to begin something. The phrase comes from football, where games start with a kick.

Let's go straight to the action. Timmy's parents have just told him that he has exactly one hour to complete the task. Right now he's putting dirty clothes in the hamper. Nice! Timmy is **kicking off** this contest in style.

Learning Box

Getting the hang of it means to learn how to do something. This idiom may come from surfing. Surfing is tough. How do you get better at it? Well, you have to hang onto the surfboard . . . with your toes.

Wait! It looks like Timmy is **getting the hang of it**. The blanket is down. Nice job, Timmy! Isn't this amazing, sports fans?

Learning Box

To meet one's match means to come across someone who is equally good at something, perhaps even better. This idiom is from one-on-one sports such as boxing, where a contest between two players is called a match. If you meet your match, it's going to be a long, tough competition.

Uh-oh, perhaps I spoke too soon. Timmy is trying to make his bed. The blanket and sheets are all twisted up. Folks, this could get ugly. Has Timmy **met his match**?

Learning Box

Get into the swing means to become comfortable with something. This idiom calls to mind golf, a sport in which it takes a while to learn how to swing the clubs properly.

He quickly moves on to gathering stinky socks. Smart choice, Timmy! He's starting to **get into the swing** of things.

Learning Box

Slam dunk is an idiom used to describe a task that is super-easy. The phrase comes from basketball. What happens when a basketball player with the ball breaks away from the other team? Since it's an easy shot now, the player often jumps high and slams the ball right into the basket.

Thunk!

He picks an easy task. Timmy takes an old apple core off his nightstand. He tosses it in the trashcan. Wowie, that was a **slam dunk**!

Learning Box

Drop the ball means to make a mistake. This idiom comes from sports such as baseball and football, where dropping the ball is an error and lets your teammates down.

Hold on, folks. Timmy is sitting down to read the comic book he found under his bed. He was doing so well. I can't believe it! Timmy seems to have really **dropped the ball** here.

Learning Box

Sail through is an idiom that means to succeed quickly and easily. The phrase comes from the sport of sailing, of course. It's one of those idioms that can really paint a picture in your mind.

Yes indeed, sports fans. Timmy looks like he is going to **sail through** this room cleanup. I don't think he'll have any problem finishing in one hour.

6   C

Learning Box

Clear another hurdle is an idiom that means to get past something that's in your way. It comes from track and field, where you have to "clear" (that's a word for *jump over*) a whole row of wooden frames (known as *hurdles*).

Now, Timmy is putting all his books back on the shelf. He's **cleared another hurdle**. Amazing! He may just finish in time.

Learning Box

Skating on thin ice means taking a foolish risk. It's from ice-skating and it's another of those idioms that paints a vivid picture. What might happen if a person skates on thin ice? It's a dangerous thing to try, right?

Oh no! Timmy's parents are back. They are reminding Timmy that he doesn't have much time. They have just told him that he's **skating on thin ice**.

8   D

Learning Box

Behind the eight ball comes from a type of billiards game where you knock the balls into the pockets in number order, but must save the eight ball for last. What if a ball you need to hit is behind the eight ball? That would mean you are in a bad situation with little hope of achieving your goal.

Good news, sports fans! Timmy has returned to cleaning. But now he has only 15 minutes left. Will Timmy finish in time? He's really **behind the eight ball**.

Be a Sport!

Help Timmy Talbot cross the finish line by finishing his sports idioms!

Choose a word from the box to complete each sentence correctly. Then write your answers in the crossword puzzle.

hurdle

wire

kick

skating

bowled

swing

sail

dunk

eight

Across

3. A very easy task is a slam _____.

4. Someone who is stunned and amazed is _____ over.

7. Someone who's running out of time is getting down to the _____.

8. Someone who's taking a foolish risk is _____ on thin ice.

Down

1. To succeed quickly at something is to _____ through it.

2. Getting past something that's in your way is clearing a _____.

5. Someone who's in a bad position is behind the _____ ball.

6. To learn how to do something is to get into the _____ of things.

9. To _____ off something means to begin it.

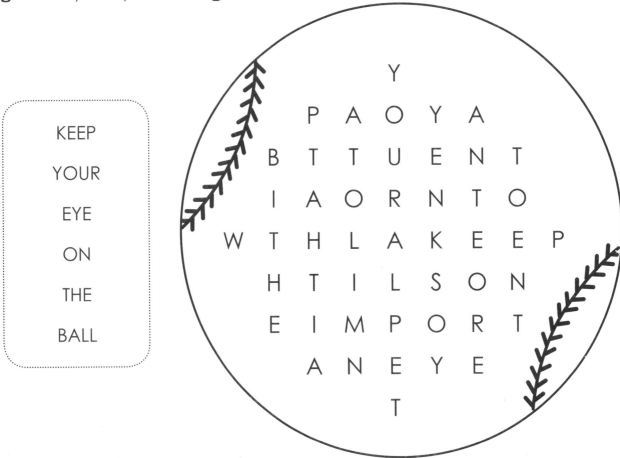

Baseball Blast

Have a ball and bust this puzzle wide open!

Read the words in the box from top to bottom. Have you ever heard this sports idiom? Find and circle each word in the puzzle. Words can go across, down, or on a diagonal.

KEEP

YOUR

EYE

ON

THE

BALL

```
                    Y
         P  A  O  Y  A
         B  T  T  U  E  N  T
         I  A  O  R  N  T  O
      W  T  H  L  A  K  E  E  P
         H  T  I  L  S  O  N
         E  I  M  P  O  R  T
         A  N  E  Y  E
                    T
```

Now bust the code! Write the uncircled letters in order (going across, from top to bottom) on the blanks below. Then read the message to see the idiom's meaning!

__ __ __   __ __ __ __ __ __ __

__ __ __ __   __ __   __ __ __ __ __ __

Answers

ANIMAL IDIOMS

Shirley Holmes, Animal Detective (page 19)

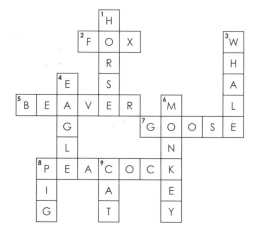

Animal Crackers! (page 20)

1. B; 2. E; 3. K; 4. N; 5. S

Solution: She thinks they're the bee's knees! (Something that's the bee's knees is absolutely marvelous.)

HUMAN BODY IDIOMS

Dry Gulch Is Bone-Dry! (page 25)

1. toes; 2. foot; 3. arm; 4. face; 5. heart; 6. bury; 7. shoulder; 8. ears

Solution: They're a sight for sore eyes! (If something is a sight for sore eyes, it is a pleasure or a relief to see.)

Stretch Your Mind! (page 26)

1. M; 2. U; 3. S; 4. C; 5. L; 6. E

Solution: muscle

WEATHER IDIOMS

Darla the Superstar (page 31)

1. made in the shade; 2. dry spell; 3. don't have the foggiest; 4. bolt out of the blue; 5. chasing rainbows; 6. every cloud has a silver lining; 7. dancing up a storm; 8. once in a blue moon

Stormy Weather (page 32)

Solution: An improbable event won't happen again.

COLOR IDIOMS

Color Confusion (page 37)

1. blue; 2. gold; 3. purple; 4. yellow; 5. colors; 6. white; 7. green; 8. red; 9. gray; 10. black

Solution: Because they talk a blue streak! (To talk a blue streak means to speak quickly and for a long time, sometimes to the point of annoying others.)

The Color Code (page 38)

1. C; 2. R; 3. A; 4. Y; 5. O; 6. N; 7. S

Solution: crayons

Answers

FEELINGS IDIOMS

Don't Be Cross! (page 43)

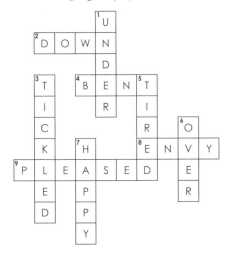

Moody Matt McKay (page 44)

1. C; 2. D; 3. E; 4. N; 5. O; 6. S

Solution: He's always having second thoughts! (If you're having second thoughts, you are reconsidering something and possibly changing your mind about it.)

FOOD IDIOMS

Who Is Pat Bodean? (page 49)

1. nut; 2. bananas; 3. pickle; 4. pie; 5. sardines; 6. potato; 7. cheese; 8. apple; 9. cucumber; 10. peas; 11. cookie; 12. beans

Solution: They think she takes the cake!

(Something or someone who takes the cake is the most outstanding or the best.)

A Milky Mystery (page 50)

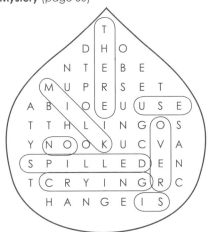

Solution: Don't be upset about things you can't change.

CLOTHING IDIOMS

Kevin Caruso's Cruise Line (page 55)

1. bee in your bonnet; 2. put on your thinking cap; 3. knock your socks off; 4. shaking in your boots; 5. ace up your sleeve; 6. hanging by a thread; 7. eat my hat

Let's Play Dress-Up! (page 56)

1. C; 2. O; 3. S; 4. T; 5. U; 6. M; 7. E

Solution: costume

SPORTS IDIOMS

Be a Sport! (page 61)

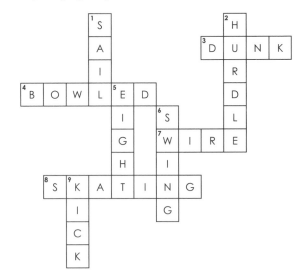

Baseball Blast (page 62)

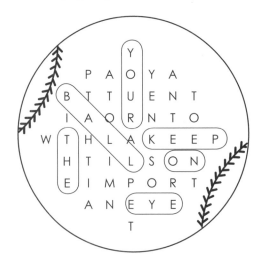

Solution: Pay attention to what is important.

Idiom Tales Teaching Guide • 64